Immortal Wreckage

ALSO BY WILL STONE

POETRY (ALL FROM SHEARSMAN BOOKS)

Glaciation (2015; 1st edition, Salt Publishing, 2007)
Drawing in Ash (2015; 1st edition, Salt Publishing, 2011)
The Sleepwalkers (2016)
The Slowing Ride (2020)

TRANSLATIONS

Les Chimères – Gérard de Nerval Shearsman Books (2018; 1st edition,
Menard Press 1999)
To the Silenced – Selected Poems of Georg Trakl Arc Publications (2005)
Journeys – Stefan Zweig Pushkin Press (2019; 1st edition, Hesperus
Press, 2010)
Rilke in Paris – Rainer Maria Rilke & Maurice Betz Pushkin Press
(2019; 1st edition, Hesperus Press, 2012)
On the End of the World – Joseph Roth Pushkin Press (2019; 1st edition,
Hesperus Press, 2013)
Nietzsche – Stefan Zweig Pushkin Press (2020; 1st edition, Hesperus
Press, 2013)
Poems – Émile Verhaeren Arc Publications (2013)
Montaigne – Stefan Zweig Pushkin Press (2015)
Messages from a Lost World – Stefan Zweig Pushkin Press (2016)
Poems – Georges Rodenbach Arc Publications (2017)
The Art of the City – Rome, Florence, Venice Pushkin Press (2018)
Surrender to Night – Collected Poems of Georg Trakl Pushkin Press (2019)
Encounters and Destinies, A Farewell to Europe – Stefan Zweig Pushkin
Press (2020)
Poems to Night – Rainer Maria Rilke Pushkin Press (2020)
Nietzsche in Italy – Guy de Pourtalès Pushkin Press (2022)
Bruges-la-Morte – Georges Rodenbach Wakefield Press (2022)
Letters around a Garden – Rainer Maria Rilke Seagull Books (2024)
Conversations with Rilke – Maurice Betz Pushkin Press (2025)

Immortal Wreckage

Will Stone

Shearsman Books

First published in the United Kingdom in 2024 by
Shearsman Books
P.O. Box 4239
Swindon
SN3 9FN

Shearsman Books Ltd Registered Office
30–31 St. James Place, Mangotsfield, Bristol BS16 9JB
(this address not for correspondence)

www.shearsman.com

ISBN 978-1-84861-942-5

ACKNOWLEDGEMENTS

Firstly, I must thank the editors of the following publications in
which a number of these poems first made their appearance:
The Spectator, the *Fortnightly Review*, the *London Magazine*, *Agenda*
and *Poetry Review*. I would also like to express my gratitude to the
gifted poet and editor Katie Lehman for her generous assistance with
the editing of this collection and her ongoing support for my work.
Likewise to the creative talent that is Emma Mountcastle
for designing the compelling cover image with the assistant
technology at her disposal.

CONTENTS

I

II

For a long time now our whole civilisation has been driving with a tortured intensity that increases from decade to decade, as if towards a catastrophe: restlessly, violently, tempestuously, like a mighty river craving the end of its journey without pausing to reflect, indeed fearful of reflection… Where we live, soon no one will be able to exist.

Nietzsche

None of you has the slightest idea what a people is, and how it deteriorates into a barbarous mob. You do not yet know what a tyrannical rule is to be set up over the spirit… we may all perish, but I for one shall choose the cause for which I am going to perish; the culture of old Europe…

Burckhardt

It is not progress but repetition which characterizes the historical process…

Byung Chul Yan

I

When the blood of man counts for nothing
it is easy to make conquests...

Chateaubriand

Uncovering a European Predator

Below silver birches in the cold peat,
through a web of flesh-coloured roots
we see him, the sleeping slaughterer,
master of the zone without light.
So tightly wound yet relaxed, foetal
bald head glistening, the scale mosaic
wrong footing prey when the sun
streams wildly over this creation.
The pulse behind the head is calm,
presiding over those madly pumping
of his unprepared, cornered victims.
Most are caught in the open, fleeing
unable to outpace the quicker blood
of terror's straining pack of hounds.
Only a husk of presence, the tiny fruit
they were carrying is left behind.
He sleeps soundly by my axe head,
his dynamo hums on through winter,
running on a rich absence of empathy
and the musculature assumed at birth,
all his unknowing mother gave him
when he slipped out, soundless, and
they held up the blood painted effigy.
Carefully, gently we re-covered him
but stood unsure as over a demon child,
and I saw his life-mocking eye half open
just above the obediently rising soil,
unconcerned, deceptively listless.

Battlefield Tourism

Crows led us in, starling multitudes,
their smoke plumes dying out by Cérisy.
Lovely are the Somme's dark bends,
their embroidery of glittering marais
beneath the Belvedere de Vaux.
Stood at the edge of the empty crater
we looked down without much hope,
new information panels scattered about;
one told of a wayside shrine ripped apart,
madonna and child strangely unscathed,
wrapped in a sackcloth, bundled away.
Cars pull in effortlessly, more unload,
advance with their smart phones raised
for the performance, perhaps the last post.
Imagination keenly rises with anticipation,
the cut off contemplate catastrophe,
each returns to their vehicle ashamed.
Those gentle rises of arable all around,
each animal feeding without knowledge,
above the insidious secret of milky roots.
For we all know, have seen and felt it,
the low tile-petalled farms, hard frost
above the grey pelt, intolerable muteness.
However impressive herb-caressed crosses,
be ready with new language at the moment
a boy leader's face passes beneath the ice.

Innocent Encounter

From a photograph of Heinrich Himmler taken by
an unknown German soldier in the Ukraine, summer 1941

In a meadow heavy with the scent
of everything that blooms
without anticipation of death,
two Ukrainian peasant girls
encounter the Reichsführer SS.
Freed from their labours they smile
and greet the slight bespectacled man
who appears benign, as he gently winds
a thick grass stem around his finger.
What a beautiful land, he opines
granted you by the fortune of birth.
But they don't understand, just smile.
Yes, one could settle here, keep pigs,
and raise a strong German family...
One nods hopefully, the other laughs
and the adjutant holding his silver gloves
praises their colourful headscarves.
On iron crosses the July sun dances,
blizzards of insects over high grasses.
Farewell then, good luck!
They turn, open leather map cases.
The girls' movement parts the rushes,
later in the firelight their flushed faces
and a full moon risen to face them all,
cut to pieces by the dark rut pools.

Labyrinth without Light

See now, see in this time
how they fill the liberated spaces
where the next gleeful despot waits,
for fresh followers, lines of old soldiers
on whose breast he pins a skull fragment
selected solemnly from a velvet-lined box.
See now the unseeing pass the threshold
to calmly enter the labyrinth without light.
The accumulated hatred, venom phials,
heirlooms passed down the generations.
In which secret facility are they stored?
Grins that scalded Christ on Calvary
when the young far right speaker arises
to take advantage of streaming devices,
a malignant tree under which empathy
kneels requesting to be finished off.
In *The Triumph of Death* by Brueghel in Basel
bodies are spread-eagled, raised on wheels
before the glowing horizon, black demons
are laughing, wielding souls on prongs,
while in England immigrants are corralled,
trapped inside the Holiday Inn, prey
behind the spit-bespattered police ring.
Obeying instinctual drives, their hunters
seek sustenance beyond the dying fires,
thus allowing the quarry to emerge by 3 a.m.
wrapped in blankets and foil, survivors
who stare at whatever's left, pick their way
through reporters out of their depth,
the carefully set nooses and snares.

The Avenue of Victory

Tiergarten, Berlin 1949

All riders now receding, fading
hoofprints punched in damp sand,
the marionette theatre is boarded up,
a wooden carrousel no longer turns.
The child's heart once thudded against
the rippling glossy mane, blood pumped,
everyone laughing came around again.
But the survivor found only forms of ash,
ranked marble figures bullet-pecked,
still awaiting their ersatz requiem mass.
Between serried scorched tree stumps,
the remains of plucky vegetable plots
a too lately cherished soil betrayed.
Beyond, the colossal head of Bismarck
rudely robbed of a torso, keeled over
to face the sky with surprised eyes
bristling with bathing sparrows.

Opportunists of Genocide

Tank tracks still stitching their fold,
at dawn they emerged, dug over, sowed.
Those mud-slowed men moving west
chins stained with apple juice and ash.
Someone smiling indicates the clearing...
Amongst lupins in flower they labour,
glean from the still moving soil
all they had gripped like charms.
At dusk the brim-full wooden barrows
bobbed and scythed through the firs,
out of the village came wild dogs, the moon
found a silver comb owned by the girl who asked
of the barber, how long does it take to die?
She claimed it, plunged the teeth
into the wood smoke waves of her hair.
Now caught out by the sun, the old one
steps quickly away from the past,
briskly brushing her strip of grass
of every intruding leaf.

All That Remains

Finally un-masked, on that corner table
we talked of the murderous collective;
hollow legions, the endlessly deceived,
eyes evolved to see ahead only, not behind
new breeds refusing every loan of history,
placard shaking tribes prancing the stage
of suburban roundabouts, hate collectors,
tin pot philosophers, witch doctors, busy spiders
their prey wrapped for later in the black web.

All those chattering keys, those shining eyes,
all those screens high up in towers, in cellars,
then pillows held down with such strength
over the sleeping faces of a generation.
Yet you spoke of all this with such eloquence
and many minutes, hours, days, months
we must have remained at that table, adrift
until we finally emerged, old machinery
like those winches marooned on a Suffolk shore
that rust before a North Sea empty of fish,
like horse bones of lunar white surfacing now
in peaceful water meadows along the Volga.

Little was left for the waitress to clear away,
debris of two stale croissants, notebook pages
moulded hard into balls, premature poems
left where they fell during the retreat.
What remained after sentence was passed?
Your lipstick smudge defiant on a cup,

like the smile of a long-rejected clown,
or the patient entrusted with minor tasks
leading newcomers into the insane asylum.

Permanently Deleted

There is an ancient European necropolis,
where sports utility vehicles pass easily over
the bleached bones of Waterloo's dragoons,
the Staffordshire yeomanry of the 6th June.
Chased behind the white cliffs, we now emerge
signalling our continental arrival with a lonely bell
out of the darkness of enforced monolingualism.
In an attempt to assuage the existential misery
of our withdrawal from the European union,
I sent out friend requests to Stefan Zweig,
Emile Verhaeren and Romain Rolland,
but due to inactivity, their accounts
had been permanently deleted.

A Place to Hide

Collaborateur horizontal
hounded out of a Picardy village,
her bleeding cheek and black eye
forever in newsreel colour footage
below trucks of laughing yanks,
borne east on furies of road dust.
Falling against the grey trunk
where thin bark had peeled back,
she registered what was still alive,
her blood smear left an inscription
none read on the plane tree's ivory flesh.
From the skilled hunter all seek escape;
school children ran to the confession box,
over smouldering cassocks and we stand
before the altar of Oradour-sur-Glane
glutted with testimony, unable to kneel
for the grotesque solemnity of prayer
next to a tiny pram's skeletal remains.

Black Hole

In Siberia men of ash
move through the forest.
They know from childhood
every animal path and clearing,
where bee orchids once signalled
and the sun spoke tenderly.
Raised to be skilled hunters, now
they are the victims of predators,
wolf packs of flame, wildfires,
so they run to the remaining green
flail wildly at the earth as if enraged,
while their wives eat frugally alone.
The pinioned sense the perfection
of this snare, the trapped human eyes
that with each counter move of darkness,
go on seeking the light foraged
from dying stars.

Cancelled

In sweat-soaked bloody lace
the scent of lavender long spent,
pressed against each other like herring
in carts and tumbrels that lurch as then
into the crowd's ever widening maw.
Or shorn of braces, medals, insignia
holding up their trousers before Judge Friesler,
who snaps, waves his white reaper's claw.
Speech severed, the verdict an avalanche
triggered by inadvertent movement,
a frozen deer that incautiously warmed
and left the glade, the weak picked off
at the ragged edge of a panicking herd.
Or one led from a tiny cell in Poperinghe
to splintered post, routine deliveries,
the giggling secretaries sent out are back
laden with baguettes and brioches.
Or rows of meat hooks shining online,
where dangle the careless and nonchalant
explaining, justifying, quivering apology,
forced into an enclosure of wilderness,
so the pack can relish the yelping pursuit,
lusting for the command when they can
tear the exhausted prey to pieces.

Diagnosis of Anxiety

Each night on news at ten we watch
the *fossoyeur* powdered white with lime
calmly read the tally by the excavation.
Accounts have been adequately kept.
Mice in cornfields, selected, fear death
for they have a heart of finite beats
and you cannot forget those Brussels rats
who, long-lived in the ruin's foundations,
when nakedly exposed by the digger's jaw
horribly span around each other like eels.
Leaves long settled on the Langerei canal
are moved by the passage of royal swans,
they turn, the amber, the ochre, the lime
priceless gemstones set awhile in darkness
along the quiet Pottererie in Bruges.
But like a wary animal you maintained
a distance from that hard-engraved line,
mourners in the old Brussels cemetery,
far enough not to hear a woman's hand
suddenly clench in an unfamiliar glove.
On the cobbled avenue darker with ice
three crows were labouring, black pistons
going powerfully at something
impossible to identify.

Living Dolls

Placed on a pile tenderly
as if to encourage brief sleep,
or easily torn from a tiny fist –
a hundred, a thousand, ten thousand
companions and twice the number
of unseeing eyes made of glass.
No child parent would return
to reclaim their mannequin infant,
no cry of recognition, no reaching out
to lift them lovingly from the dune.
The hut where they were taken
was cool and dark, on dry shelves
they placed the orphans head to toe
layered like sardines to save space.
The laundry girl was conscripted
because she could knit and sew
new outfits for the naked; dresses,
uniforms, sailor suits and blouses.
The master made his selection;
This one shall be a little SS man,
a festive gift for my son back home,
Christmas is for family as you know.
Carefully she buttoned them,
smoothed the new frocks down,
laid her changelings carefully
like fine wines nestled in straw,
and they arrived the saved by
Deutsche Bahn to Frankfurt,
Leipzig, Heidelberg, Cologne.

Shadows in a Landscape

Some become shadow on snow,
reach existence later in a dark room
as nameless monochrome effigies,
still with wedding rings on chains
around their necks, a family deported
their smallest child burrowed deep in furs,
and the toboggan the rest all heaved.
No-one in this photograph survived.

Poorly equipped and in a crevasse
too deep for ropes, we late ones wait
grouped like Goya's squatting lunatics,
global shoals now conjoining, drawn
towards and away from great changes
welling determinedly like the drowned
just beneath the suddenly frozen surface.

I remember that horse being fettled
given feed by the beguinage of Bruges,
seeing my tiny reflection sink un-rescued
into the deepest onyx well of its eye.
How much time is left to launch our love?
Prisoners still issue thanks to their last sun
whose embers briefly warm the bars.

Ghost Road to Culbone

Between landslides fresh and old
the shades pass, on the ghost road
their grey feet stir cowslip, primrose,
leave no imprint on the virgin fern.
Silence travels this way to Culbone.
Lord King's woodlands long outgrown,
canopies of ash, beech, maple, cedar,
their dark sails slacken and stiffen
rarely sinking a sleepy well of light.
The years and all who looked west
to shores of Glenthorne and Embelle
from the laurel smothered lookout,
unrecorded by wayfarers, secret now.
The philosopher's walk, steps erased
long overlaid by the creak of trunks
condemned, forced by winter storms
to submit, even while holding each other.
Denied or resisting a grave, all walk on
beneath our own tread, they whisper
between bee orchids and fritillaries,
through acres of wild rhododendron
appear finally at the brash young cliff,
gazing out wildly at what fell away,
recoiling from the raw ochre flesh
of the new scree, the nescience
of doomed saplings.

The Conviction of Claire Goll

Condemned
for the black cloth she spun,
and a generation of spiders
similarly veined with that poison
rushed down from webs to learn.
In Transnistria no bones were left,
scavengers ran with those prizes,
into the forests of firs while the roped
women and girls whispering psalms
calmly slipped into icy Pomeranian lakes.
On the shortest day mid-century
snow fell early, a pencil stub stopped
mid way through a journal entry.
And beneath every fresh layer,
however heavy, however light
denied rescuers can still make out
the shining head of the hatchet.

Heidelbergensis

Humans down to 1280 souls for 117,000 years...
Yet still the biped endured, their cunning, eyes
gazing at fish spinning in rainbow arcs of spray,
feeling superior to the fungi, molluscs and algae.
So was laid the shining casket of Silicon Valley
and new promises through a rippling wall of silk.
Each was seduced or became disorientated, ran
onto the upturned spikes, the even less fortunate
stoked the pyres after the departure of the 'artist'.
As anti-depressants cascade from shifting trays
the robot dog's crooked leg flexes grotesquely.
Man finally stood up in order to cross the glade,
the prairie, the plain, the steppe, the lowland valley
to reach upwards for fruit, so they had claimed,
but in truth it was to better slaughter the animals
they had watched for so long through leaves,
creatures they admired and had grown to love.

Downfall

One evening mid-summer
downfall for the red ant colony.
You watched the carefully placed eggs,
tumble in chaos from the fresh cliff edge,
streams of workers sent insane
ran silent screaming into the gravel.
Their collapse, as ours, happened
to the steady breathing of machines,
no reserves, no back-up generation.
Are we nothing more than those naked
self-disinterred souls of the Flemish Primitives
cantering hopefully across lawns to Michael
or flinching away from the demon's fork?
Each searches now for a way through,
even as the rib vault of the scree wolf
now on the move, swells at the fresh scent
and bands of leaderless feral children
burst from fir forests, into the decadence
seared pedestrian zones of Brussels,
they trot on makeshift spikes and poles,
the bloodied heads of those who called for
renewed dialogue, calm and restraint.

II

Because nowhere now is an Immortal to be seen in the skies...

Hölderlin

II

Gift of Light

On the no 39 bus, at the lights
before the Bibliothèque Royale,
it happened, a splinter of light
found the mother's human hand
moving towards her child's head,
masked face unknown in a pram.
Her hand alone was blessed, chosen,
as it fussed nimbly with the blankets
then motionless, still as a bird in foliage
rested on the pale peeping brow.
That light was holy, unacknowledged,
it spoke then and never again,
the mark was hers but meant for all,
like the song of the old man at Matins
wrapped around the pillar of the basilica.
His weakening body clamped there
by a muscle of will, nothing more.
As the service ended he dropped,
a last petal from the spent stem
and the young white-robed nun
who suddenly seemed more tender,
put out the candles one by one.

Corner Shop

Friday afternoons in all seasons,
when blossoms leapt from gardens
only to slow in damp asphalt scent,
or that October wind, cloud-paled
shook the early dead leaves in,
you held up a warm sixpence
and she turned to the shelves,
to face the rank of misted jars.
A toy tin shovel dusted white,
tipped into a tiny paper bag
swung briskly once to secure
the cache of sugary amber rocks.
The bell over the door rang wearily,
as out you slipped with a scent of
counter, of drawers and shelves,
of dust and unlived window air.
So it vanished, became a home
we passed on our way to school,
mausoleum, that off-white wall
where the outline of the old door
proved itself as cracks in plaster,
insistent, yet never quite enough
like those across ice left by one
drifting beneath, determined to live
but who cannot break through.

Set Aside

Once we were all fresh, flushed with appetite,
like bright young perch hooked without bait –
we just saw something gleaming and acted.
And even then, unhooked, gored, wounded
we swam strongly in the keep net like the rest.
Now we keep still, terrified by the resumption
of some pain, check in on our weals and scars,
intricate patterns in flesh left by the flails of loss.
Now we are faded like field edge grass, set aside
in the hope that all the diminishing species,
insects, reptiles, and song birds will find us.
Strong young crops rise all around, the blade
of the combine whips past and stubble is left.
We look out at the broken seasons, they go on
dragging their spears till strength gives out.
The never sated crow returns to the carcass.
We remain for what purpose? The condemned
pheasant's twitching face drops down into us,
the moorhen leads her diminishing brood
over our lines, and the sparrow hawk rustles
like a child's kite high above, but breaks off
apparently unconvinced, to search elsewhere
for incautious signs of movement.

Njm

For Emma M.

Not remembrance
for I *see* him there in the window,
anchored as he was, eyes closed,
relishing everything familiar,
the reassurance of the room.
Then another day in his home,
the sun would stretch him out
upon the old cardboard box
as on a pedestal behind plate glass.
From the garden I watched him there
impressively idle and innocent,
still, silent, without expectance.

Sometimes he stepped out gingerly
as one from a rest home lounge,
inspected a frond, a blade of grass,
sniffed the air, but furtively,
then confused, went back in.
That slow-moving elderly boy
lacked all urge to bite and claw,
save when his teeth were brushed,
lacked all urge to harm and hunt.
His one kill in error, a house spider,
who, inadvertently disabled
was no longer in a position
to become a new friend.

Late evening, he made his move,
panther sway along the sofa back,
climbing down with a child's stealth
to make a nest on my chest, his face
opposite mine, but so close, at my throat
paws neatly together, bound in silk.
Gentleness was his sole guardian,
and even as the tide trapped him
there on the diminishing shore,
he, unaware, contented, still warm
slept on in their basket of loving arms.

Love under the Heat Dome

For Kathleen Rooney in Chicago

The fresh lovers saw only themselves.
Their powerful isolation, their future pain
set carefully as cold rings in warm velvet.
They still met in the park of the metropolis
at the appointed hour under the heat dome.
Beyond the shimmering serpentine fleets
of black military vehicles an AI despatched,
they made basic attempts to stay human.
Barely clothed, on a hot graffitied bench
they turned sideways to face each other,
a residual timidity made him courteous
and she laughed with him, longing for ice.
A siren sounded to which none responded,
a grey mongrel dog, weary and dehydrated
flicked its tail under a dusty evergreen shrub.
They exchanged little gifts, charming things,
then a feral howl erupted from the folly
at one end of the pond, dealers occupied.
She knew street walkers came here at night
and took their clients behind the beeches
just a few yards from the path, discarding
their detritus beneath, which could not be
absorbed by the soil, but remained there
a scrawny piecemeal script, alien.
Awkwardly yet tenderly they embraced,
unhesitatingly handing over their own eyes.
No one knew how they had supported life
in this single moment, then it was over

the branches of their bower trees clattered
as the metal rain swept in, insect carapaces
crowds in eddies around the park
the people of ash gathering, envious
of those still in possession of a shadow.

First Narcissus

Traveller, I watched you
appearing on dawn's glacier,
inwardly playing with found light.
Undeviating, in steely burnished green,
your blood, the hours, the will pushing on
for that sunny flute, like a sail suddenly raised
in verticality for Helios alone.
Held fast while breezes come to prepare,
persuaded by the rearing charger of day,
you step forth calmly into late winter sun
already a tiny doll reflected in death's pupil
strangely emboldened by your unborn kin.
I saw you ride out that early March morning,
garlanded in dew beads, behind a dancing wren
guarded by two upward gazing seraphim,
like the defaced heads at rest in Porlock church
of Knight John Harrington and his lady.

Eternal Life

Slowly the leaves grow yellow and fall,
and I hear leaders of corporate empires
fully confident of achieving eternal life
for select customers in their lifetime.
But in the Aveyron in the year 1851,
most peasants the traveller encountered
expressed a sincere longing for death.

Lone swan on the Goudenhandrei
lifting off, permitted by ancient law
to tear open the pristine onyx surface,
All is spent then before ripples embalm
and the little skiffs of down are borne
beneath green and violet venetian glass.

In the chapel above Raron I light candles,
pay the franc due for each finite flame.
Our lifeboats sit too low in the water,
around us white arms break the surface,
cries slip eagerly out of the blackness,
but there are just too many to rescue,
in the end the weakening, the unprepared
can be easily fended off with an oar.

Pyres

That year when they burned the cattle
and English hedgerows were dams of lace
strangely containing a poisonous amber,
or when it finally came, the direct order
and peasants who delivered them bread
clocked the plume, closed their windows.
Deeper still, must a fallen race descend
craving virgin seams, habitable planets;
an endless rope of melancholy miners
black-oiled in sweat even before labour,
their white eyes resisting in the darkness
bright and terrible as exposed bone.

All must now catch the distant rumble.
But tentatively the first picks chip away
a shovel scrapes once, again, drills grunt,
swiftly the empty man cage ascends.
In a mahogany box, a wicker cocoon
or left on a scarred ledge bound in ropes
by the severed arches of an aqueduct,
or in an English suburban crematorium
whose disinfection protocol won praise.
    You decide…
Prayer trees grow powerfully in churches,
their pale pink cards hang on cotton threads
scrawled with sad and desperate messages.
Back and forth go the worn-out ambulances,
bellowings of recrimination, lust and hatred
it's on your clothes, in your hair, following you
everywhere, the greasy odour of collapse.

But wait child, for the first primroses
that break their journey on a western shore
to calmly leave their pale lovely whispering
about the lichened graves of Morwenstowe.
Swim strongly away from the downward
pull of the sinking vessel, from the figures
all around in disarray, the whirling drowned
ever grabbing onto you, those worn bare feet
protruding from the wood pyres
of Amritsar.

Lost Quays of Antwerp

For Sven Peeters

I had imagined they were protected
by the implacable sentinels of history,
these iron rails that lead nowhere,
these iron sheds that shelter no goods.
That winter's day the rails still shone
like new petals, frost on eaves in the sun,
as if the trolley wheels had just passed
and I saw the shade of a coal carrier
draped in a cloth sack, another bent low
under pineapples and Japanese parasols.
These images lingered there awhile
against the grey pane like weary moths,
their bright-patterned wings darkening
on the day before their extinction.

Sentence Is Passed

I am *Resident 2987*
residing in the danger zone
of Sizewell C, a new nuclear reactor.
To EDF, the constructor, I am a number
as befits a prisoner or one condemned,
perhaps held back to be finished off later
at the optimal moment, or even to be offered
as a bargaining chip in some prurient deal
brokered by a Swiss diplomat of noble birth.
My allotted number duly appears
in all correspondence, EDF publicity emails
breeze-streaming banderoles, fanfares,
glib reassurances over wildlife and trees
icily crafted by teams of EDF functionaries,
who have generously offered compensation
after expert advice and robust negotiation –
a two-way tunnel for voles and a bat station.
But alas, the barn owl's pale brushstroke
along the Sizewell belt of firs was erased.
In the village hall an exhibition to clarify…
Checked off by the smiling, reassured,
led to ranks of hard, cold, plastic chairs,
we await the volley, perform a final check
to ensure the rough white square of paper
is pinned directly over our hearts.

Lonely Sunflower Field

Astray somewhere near Lucy-en-bois,
I pass the tribe who shiver beneath crows –
charcoal heads, crowd pressing in for bread,
starving prisoners in the pen, *untermenschen*.
Perhaps the bones of a doomed chivalry
or glaciers built up this Burgundian plateau,
where sleek white turbines with cyclopean eye
wink red over the bowing bee-seekers;
those yellow haired lovers once massing
now alone, stained with summer's blood,
nobly preparing, on their way to stone.
But see, a single human heart draws near
moves at dusk within the whispering naked.
Nothing lies beyond, only a wayside cross
deprived of pilgrims, effaced, subsiding.
Though Mary is still there, the infant fruit
weightless at her breast has perished.

Green Burial

To the memory of my father
Walter Ernest Stone (1929–2020)

When the urn came to me
I bore it like precious water
through our drought-bleached land,
where I saw ribs of stricken herds
anchored into sculpture by sand
shining even whiter under a sun
that again unsheathed new blades.
Then suddenly we entered shade,
those silent courts of oak and beech
with their new green suspended,
the always burgeoning arboreal
that once protected the child I was.
Childhood, those gentle wavelets
meeting a barbed wire shore…

Boys hiding under low crab apples
tracking each other, playing war
or racing down on 'trolleys', made
of crates, rope and old pram wheels.
One winter gifted the never before
our sledges hissing over new snow,
the sweetest sound, that ice smell.
Along the parched bed of *the stream*,
I lay my father, to wait for the water,
gleaming eddies and jewel pools,
the return of blood and movement
as half a century ago at Trebarwith

when he rose powerfully from the sea,
and I swaying astride his shoulders
rode high, fearless, untouchable.

Blood Trail

Above Molland, Twitchen or by Hawkridge
you hear the hounds whine-yelping, see them
slippery as eels, visceral, forming their shoals
to loose their one shadow over the moor,
carry their current over dry-stone walls.
In the fetid snug, clumps of huntsmen
spew jokes and anecdotes, faces of ham,
their eyes glistening with laughter and
a pale film of lust, rage or derelict empathy.
The whip-carrying ladies, freshly spruced
are already mounted, fern brushed lackeys
mill around the *scum trucks*, bolted to tradition
or necessity, and further out in the constellation
orbiting sabs, Reynard's cagouled seraphim.
A hunting horn toots, haughty and defiant,
hoof din builds, dung steams on wet tarmac.
The drapes of ritual hang heavy with jewels,
blood drops set in frozen sweat of the butchered.
The hounds twist, pirouette madly, bite the air
leap powerfully to nowhere, Tally Ho!
Down the fresh hewn cliff of the new stink pit
the first of the eviscerated slides.

Todeskammer

The open mouth of a dying friend,
dark oval you watch like a tracker the sign
in the dust, then move on unrewarded.
Fishing for air, the final trawl of the lake
but nothing is found, only the form
of the diver receding darkly through reeds.
On a bedside wipe-off board
This patient would like to be known as...
Nurses chatter, a sound, a breeze
sends dead leaves scuttling into a corner.
The dark-haired Jewess who died young,
her portrait found in a Brussels cemetery
unnamed, unremembered, unknown
forced by weathering into another;
sorceress, mad woman or spectre.
Establish a perimeter, hold the line.
Frost on frozen wires, you grip them,
knowing you will not break free.

Immortal Wreckage

A souvenir of Old Vézelay

What silence could have once existed,
to keep the doves so still in their niches.
The wire hum of the cloister bats
ushered in the last dark-robed monk
who had climbed along decayed walls
of fortress towers, massive and rooted.
No neat arrow slits but brute gouges,
rough apertures lacking legend or faces.

Terraces pitched under rigging of vine,
extinct gates bled their rust into weeds
and trails of cats around subsiding tombs
that scatter their bleached litter of bones.
The elderly nun sits under the lime tree
and selects another bead of patience
from the shade, enfolds it in her palm
like a found coin. She at least is saved.

Sunflower fields brightly enclosing
concede to the scattered lamps of Asquins.
A few pray in the chapel of *La Cordelle*,
a German woman leans into the cross,
pipes and folk violin rise by a scented bush.
In the narthex of the Madeleine, pilgrims,
faith's sailors who outswam the currents
or wrecked were miraculously picked up
kneel as one, gaze on the eternal
rippling folds of the redeemer.

Hymn to Beauty

After C. Baudelaire

In the supermarket for spectacles
I noticed the young woman who
assisted me in choosing my varifocals
possessed a central European accent.
I enquired where she hailed from.
I'm from Poland, she said brightly,
Katowice, a town close to Auschwitz.
Her slender fingers tapped confidently
on the keys, her grey-green eyes flashed,
darted a little too hungrily, longingly
about the screen, seeking the best deal,
eyes I had seen before set in the head
of a blood-ruffed husky in harness
straining powerfully across a sea of ice.
Suddenly she leaned back in her chair
as a colleague passed, they conversed.
The resulting curve in her torso directly
recalled a work by Georges Minne,
a gifted Belgian artist barely known here.
It was impossible then and there to accept
that this pale face, so pure, harbouring
some indefinable yet plausible gene
suggestive of immortality, permanence,
was in fact a casually applied garment
for the crude skull, its two deep sockets
tarns dark and still with dead water,
terrifyingly response less, lying in wait,
rejected toy at the bottom of the box,

which one day rises, victorious, vengeful,
to be placed carefully alongside or on top
of those you find in alcoves beneath Palermo
or in pyramids and piles set at intervals
along the tunnels into which tourists slip
willingly, chattering their chilly bravado,
in Paris, beneath Denfert Rochereau.

Pynes in Memoriam

In Epping I was born, and before me
Pynes the little department store,
that smelled of polish, wood cabinets
beeswax, shoe leather and wool.
I loved hiding there, in the secret
dark corners between draperies,
spaces offering stillness, protection.
I loved its two narrowing entrances
deep set in the vintage vitrine, outside
you were somehow inside, already in.
Now here is where Pynes once was,
and nothing remains but the proof
of those two narrowing entrances,
their fine mosaic flooring spelling *Pynes*,
unmolested, curiously preserved,
noble gesture, celebrated miracle.
But no… humiliation and mockery
for they lead to a void, a chain bistro,
where in the old Pynes window
teens graze on their upheld phones.
The mosaic beauties wait patiently,
mournfully dusted with yellowed leaves
and briefly my reflection in the door,
the spectre who cannot enter, unnoticed
by identically dressed waitresses
revolving in a brittle space.

Munch and the Art Critics

Munch is back, the storehouse raided,
all is recycled, pressed back into service.
Mental disintegration on his part offered
a certain protective against this type,
against those spilling from the future
clothed differently yet the same,
humming around the seer like horse flies
attracted by sweat and fame, so casually
employing words like *solitude* and *melancholia*.
In every review they pun on *The Scream*,
painstakingly unwind the barbed wire
from his body, check manifold wounds,
probe them knowingly like surgeons.
You can find them afterwards at the
pub around the corner from the RA,
leaving the bar beaming, bearing
slopping pints of his blood on trays.

The Desecrated Valley

For Bruce Mueller in San Francisco

In Muzot one did not speak
of Villas Mercier or Ruffieux,
vulgar pile of a swiss industrialist,
those Disney towers above Sierre.
The poet caressed his own walls
fully ripened now seven centuries,
stooped to touch the first anemone
turning it tenderly to the spring light,
which had arrived a little too hastily.
Now from the valley of the Rhone
towards all these marooned towers
a colossal golden M upward grows,
and on-line air-conditioned occupants
speed past on the velvet-lined road
to Crans Montana, past squat concrete
blockhaus bungalows with security
facial recognition cameras installed,
seeding their kin in ancient meadows
where once vine workers the poet knew
led donkeys with their baskets of jewels.
The excited ladies returning from Italy
no longer climb up from the Bellevue
in suggested sensible walking shoes,
competing to spy the single poplar,
exclamation mark! his faithful herald.
Gone the quiet walks to vineyard chapels
leaving wild posies for a rustic virgin,
in the cathedral of Valère above Sion,

or at a tiny table under Muzot's fruit trees
recalling those of the endangered café
on Orta's Sacre Monte, all ivory linen
and late sun on silver, a whispering
from the cell of the condemned.

The Dedication of Otto Dix

Nūllum magnum ingenium sine mixtūrā dēmentiae fuit
No great talent without an element of madness
—Seneca

Obeying his severe master *Truth*,
the painter Dix was willingly interred
and by candle light avidly studied
the Capuchin mummies of Palermo.
There he could not hear the crowd above
bawling, crowing, protractedly carousing,
who would shun his fifty etchings of war,
would not accept that in no man's land
wild flowers could germinate and bloom
out of a mouldering corpse's cloven head.
With mannequins in niches he conversed,
the silence of these survivors sound advice.
Priests in their desiccated tunics looked on,
a grimy sand timer upheld in the claw of one.
He sketched, reflecting on the gifted young,
the new heroic handful up there, pushing on,
feeling a way round the limits of their time,
like roe deer in a line, desperate to slip through
not succumb, moving on then slowing, gentle
smoke drifting across woods of lichened oaks
until the sunlit glades are dark once more.
And he recalled how he had sat amongst them
admiring their alert, suddenly hopeful faces
shining towards the speaker, and his awareness
of the pale skeletal branch behind his speech
on which a line of corvid preened, squabbled,

suddenly lifted off as one and settled again.
One day he emerged, flame from the hole,
the sheaf of drawings tight under his arm,
bound with cord from a Papal robe.

Despair of an Expert in His Field

In departure lounges, waiting rooms,
perhaps Antwerp, Basel or Cologne,
he mentally checks how secure his domain.
But beyond the siege machines assemble,
the young upstarts, with their blitzkrieg
social media campaigns, their shining eyes
and eel-like movements at launch parties.
Everywhere now the same febrile movement,
missions, strategies for instant achievement,
workshop facilitators prancing at conferences.
In a smooth holding pattern they wait to land
the well-crafted witticism, like searchlights
their keen eyes play over the fleets of rivals.
Yours was more an old trench war, slugging
in testy spats on the letters page of the TLS.
You inveigled your way into private libraries,
into vaults, the carapaces of country houses.
You grafted, gleaned a coveted professorship
and all the time your subject was in chains,
travelling with you like an obedient bear.
And so you erected the red warning signs –
private property, no access, trespassers keep out!
They called you the doyen, specialist, expert
and you raced to culture shows like a paramedic,
to prove you always knew more, were far closer
to this pulse than any living being on earth.
But now it's over, so suddenly did the dusk fall
and you are distanced, a disgraced herdsman
who descended from the high pastures alone

to end paring mountain cheese mournfully,
somewhere in Piedmont or the Engadine.

Resistance in Paris

In order to see
Rilke closed his eyes
Monique Saint-Hélier said.
In order to speak he employed
the costly services of silence.
How illness surprised them all
lying in wait in dark hedgerows.
When death stepped into the road
a slender white figure, a stranger
asking for directions to the community.
Then some form that thrives unseen
and is only imagined, changes direction
from that place no light reaches
at the deepest part of the ocean.
So she was left by the open window
as doctors and machines crowded in.
Paris stole through like a cat at night,
over-scented, quivering, mewling
for human warmth and new prey,
unknowing of the love she had
already exhausted on that creature
exploring every room restlessly,
ignoring the remembered portraits
she was desperately sculpting,
within a narrowing shaft of light.

Notes

I

Uncovering a European Predator

This poem draws on the period in the 1980s when I worked as a volunteer for the British Trust of Conservation Volunteers, clearing silver birch and scrub in Epping Forest. Sometimes our pickaxes would unearth slumbering adders coiled in the roots still in their winter hibernation. The poem also refers to the recent tragic and needless war in the Ukraine and its perpetrator.

Innocent Encounter

The poem concerns a rare colour photograph of Heinrich Himmler and members of his staff enjoying an amicable encounter with a pair of Ukrainian peasant girls in local dress standing in a pasture somewhere behind the lines during the Russian campaign of 1941. It is an image replete with suggestion and mystery, in some tangible sense a suspension of reality. The girl's presumed ignorance of who this slight bespectacled man before them is and what he will leave to history is quietly devastating.

Labyrinth without Light

The poem is concerned with the way the past repeats, the same tyrannical mechanism, just updated to a new generation of the wilfully blind. The final part of the poem refers to a recent news report about immigrants fleeing brutal mobs of far-right xenophobes in an English coastal town, and having to be corralled into a nearby Holiday Inn for their own protection. The apocalyptic scene is equated with those in Brueghel's famous painting which can be seen in the Kunstmuseum, Basel.

THE AVENUE OF VICTORY

The comparison of pre-war and post-war Berlin is the subject of this poem. I have always been curious as to the origins of the industriousness, ingenuity and determinedness of the German survivors who scraped a life out of almost nothing amidst the rubble and detritus of their thousand-year Reich. The desperate vegetable plots in the Tiergarten overwhelmed by destruction in the Russian attack echo those planted rather more confidently in London parks and gardens during the early part of the war and which Stefan Zweig celebrated in his essay 'Gardens in Wartime' from 1940. (See Stefan Zweig, *Journeys*, Pushkin Press, 2019).

OPPORTUNISTS OF GENOCIDE

This poem relates to a disturbing revelation of avarice and absence of empathy, which occupies a place at the very limits of human understanding. It concerns the site of the notorious Treblinka extermination camp in Poland when following the war local Polish peasantry feverishly dug over the ground hoping to find Jewish gold. Mostly they found human remains and the odd worthless utilitarian or decorative item such as a brooch, a child's doll, or comb. It apparently mattered little to these grave robbers that 700,000 to 800,000 innocent Jewish victims had been murdered on the site over a period of just fifteen months as part of Operation Reinhard, the Nazi programme to exterminate Polish Jewry. I recalled a line from the poet Georg Trakl (1887–1914) 'das grässliche Lachen des Golds' (The horrible laughter of gold…)

A PLACE TO HIDE

This poem was inspired by disturbing colour newsreel footage from the end of the war which shows an abused woman, possibly a prostitute or collaborator, wandering dazedly at the side of a road in France as trucks swollen with Allied soldiers roar past. It also pertains to my experience many years ago in the church of the notorious ruined village of Oradour-sur-Glane, razed by an SS Division heading to Normandy in June 1944 and preserved after the war by President de Gaulle as a permanent memorial to the barbarism visited on civilians by a genocidal war.

BLACK HOLE

A poem which refers to the extensive wildfires in Siberia a few years ago, and a news report of the fire-fighting forestry men who volunteered to stem the relentless tide of flames. There was something heroic and tragic, Sisyphean in their exhausting and impossible task, and the toll on them, their wives and families was tremendous, yet quickly forgotten in the renewed onslaught of even more disturbing news events.

DIAGNOSIS OF ANXIETY

During the Covid crisis I became increasingly disturbed and sickened by the nightly BBC news bulletins, updating the casualty figures in a relentless monotonous fashion, prattling statistics who were in fact people – like those watching or the newsreaders themselves – who died due to government negligence in the most horrible ways. In society nothing is ever clarified but is rather veiled because to reveal absolute truth would cause panic or even some kind of revolt. This tally, repeated *ad nauseam* each night, was in essence, it seemed to me, a form of mass hypnotism, of control. Yet it was simply accepted by the majority without further reflection and then its abrupt termination, though cases and deaths continued for some time, was not questioned.

LIVING DOLLS

The poem was inspired by the 2017 documentary *Four Sisters* by Claude Lanzmann, the director of *Shoah* (1985). One of the four survivors of Nazi tyranny had been sent to the extermination camp of Sobibor in Poland where she was conscripted by the SS overseers as a seamstress. Her job was to make new clothes for the dolls of the Jewish child victims, which were given a makeover, recycled so to speak, and sent to Germany as dolls for German children. The SS men in the camp ordered dolls for their own children and had them dressed as to their taste. This account is quite possibly the most disturbing of all the testimony I have heard over some forty years of studying Holocaust literature in all its genres. But aside from the grotesquery and inherent evil, it holds something terribly significant concerning the German mania for making use of every offcut from their extermination programme, even a lowly child's doll. For here they go as far as to recreate another doll from the expunged one, a new being from the old. Why then one might be tempted to ask, in an admittedly futile venture, could they not recreate a Nazi child from a Jewish one, instead of just murdering them? Essentially the answer is because their doctrine was so explicitly exterminatory, so purely radical in the racial decision of to 'live or not to live', that even when to do the opposite would be more productive or even help perpetuate their regime, they returned to default. In this they hold a unique position in history and this is why 'reassuringly' comparing the Nazi genocide to the Soviet or any other throughout history proves futile.

SHADOWS IN A LANDSCAPE

The poem began after seeing a photograph of a Jewish family. during winter on a snow-covered Polish landscape, being deported to an unknown destination in the East. Their possessions are packed onto a primitive sled which they push. The smallest child sits atop the bundles. Their fate is unknown, but the odds confirm they would almost certainly have perished. But in the photographic record of that moment where the family unit is in motion, staring out as one into the unknown, they are still together, supporting each other, facing the elements with resolution. The poem seeks to highlight our explicit vulnerability even when we feel relatively safe.

THE CONVICTION OF CLAIRE GOLL

Claire Goll (1890–1977) was a German-French writer who grew up in Munich and, in protest at the war, emigrated to Switzerland in 1916. After the war she moved to Paris where in 1921 she married the poet Yvan Goll and published her stories, poems, and novels in French. Following the death of her husband in 1950, she dedicated her life to promoting his work. The 'Goll affair' as it came to be known, was caused by her insistence that the great German language poet Paul Celan was guilty of plagiarising her husband's works, though if anything it was the other way around. Celan's anxiety and sense of persecution increased significantly in the aftermath of Claire

Goll's unjust claims, which hastened his death by drowning in the Seine in April 1970.

HEIDELBERGENSIS

This poem, scrupulously informed by science, asks if it was at that moment so many millennia back in our history when man raised himself onto two legs and became a biped that everything started to go awry.

II

GIFT OF LIGHT

This poem begins and ends in contrasting atmospheres, though the two are somehow connected by the state of grace that materialises in both. It begins in a crowded bus crawling through heavy traffic in Paris and ends in the more peaceful environs of a service in 'La Madeleine', the Romanesque abbey of Vézelay in Burgundy.

LOVE UNDER THE HEAT DOME

I wrote this after the unprecedented heatwaves in Canada a few summers ago. So many more heatwaves have ravaged the earth since, but the unexpected Canadian tragedy was singularly harrowing. But this poem is not about the heatwave *per se* but about the lovers who are both united and enclosed in a space where nothing can touch them. They are like those waxen leaves off which heavy drain-drops slip and create dew-like balls, resistant to external storms. The city park, and what unfolds in and around it – the urban squalor fused with the climate emergency – is the threat to the survival of their fragile blossoming.

Eternal Life

This poem was initiated by learning of billionaires seeking eternal life through cryogenics. At the same time I had read in Graham Robb's book on France an account by a traveller passing through the Aveyron in 1851 who had found elements of the peasantry there that apparently sought the opposite course. It made me consider this obsession with living as long as possible at any cost in a terminally damaged eco-system, and the conflicting ways individuals deal with this knowledge, which leads either to bold selfless action, resigned apathy or faith in a technological miracle.

Lonely Sunflower Field

Lucy-en-bois is the delightful name of one of many delightfully named villages in Burgundy. In my first collection, *Glaciation*, I wrote the poem 'Stragglers' about a field of dead sunflowers behind my cottage in Suffolk. I revisit those left behind here 'à la française', in a more remote setting near Lucy, but closer to an army of enormous wind turbines, a strange otherworldly juxtaposition of nature and technology.

Lost Quays of Antwerp

Over the past few years, the authorities in Antwerp have taken it upon themselves to upgrade, renovate, and rebuild the whole waterfront. The entire western flank of the city adjoins the river Scheldt and its estuary enters the North Sea some miles beyond the vast labyrinthine port of Antwerp as it has done for centuries, the main artery that following the decline of Bruges created the rich modern city of trade and commerce. The old waterfront, where once liners docked and cargo ships were unloaded, has in latter decades been a memorial to its busier maritime past, the largely abandoned quays and old cranes, ornately decorated iron hangars where goods from all over the world were once stored before the modern container port came into being. The waterfront was then a tomb, but a beautiful one, with its own lonely atmosphere, and its own life, that of the past. It was the residue of what once was, with its old rails embedded in cobbles leading nowhere and photogenic empty quays. But instead of retaining this unique patina, this legacy, the city burghers in their wisdom decided to rip almost all of it up and replace such scenes with soulless concrete expanses fit for skateboarders, with a few cold metal benches being the only feature, and where one now stands exposed, searching around in vain for some meaningful anchorage. Quite why they did this remains a mystery, as at all such sites of desecration. But the majority see improvement in such schemes, those who lament complain or resist are always a minority and are most often passed over. (*See following Note*). As William Blake said 'Improvement makes straight roads, but the crooked roads without improvement are roads of genius'.

IMMORTAL WRECKAGE

The title poem here concerns again the medieval village of Vézelay, in the department of Yonne in Burgundy, whose relative dominance in my current poems may be because I have spent periods of time there over recent years and have witnessed the changes wrought. This poem is a paean to the old Vézelay, the one which was just about intact spiritually speaking before teams arrived to begin cleaning the walls and façade of the abbey and also the surrounding battlements and medieval gateways. These at my visit still wore the skin of centuries; hence they were characterful 'beings' showing their long-lived experience through that weathered outer layer, with grass and herbs sprouting between the cracks of their masonry, which met the rough, uneven ground at their feet. They were the architectural bedrock of old Vézelay, a part of the natural landscape. Then suddenly they were entirely stripped of this centuries old life over just a matter of months, and re-emerged naked, reborn, clean and white, more like models, or Disney towers, with a phalanx of neat parking machines installed at their approach. All spick and span, the new look pleased the controlling urban-minded who professed the 'renovation' was a vast improvement. Bravo! UNESCO grants well spent! But in one fell swoop they had swept away the past, their makeover having eradicated something which can never be reinstated.

Hymn to Beauty

I should perhaps have called this poem 'A Carcass', since it refers to that landmark of modernism, Baudelaire's poem 'Une Charogne', which has stayed with me since my first encounter with it as a younger man. I think of its lines often when I behold a beautiful woman, or rather a woman who stirs in me the image of beauty and more so when it is unexpected, as in this case. The reality of our fate and even that of the beautiful face commanding one's attention in the moment is overwhelming and so intolerable it must be veiled, like a corpse upon which the sheet is drawn back just an instant for identification. Baudelaire was the first to not place the sheet back.

Pynes was a small department store in the market town of Epping in Essex, where I was born and spent my earliest years. Typical of the kind that could be found then everywhere across England, it was scented with leather and wool, with polish. Lined with wood shelves, it had all manner of nooks and crannies, where a child could hide, and most crucially two old fashioned glass vitrines at the entrance, so in effect one walked past the windows to the door, as if in a short narrowing tunnel of glass. The floor of these entranceways was inlaid with beautiful mosaic tiles and at their centre was written in florid calligraphy 'Pynes', reminiscent of the Belle Epoque. These scraps of mosaic flooring are now all that remain of the original Pynes store, still advertising the name of the deceased. Pynes and a few other notable shops, now almost all extinct, symbolised the former genteel and quiet town of Epping, that is now hard to imagine ever existed, like so many other shire towns of its kind.

THE DESECRATED VALLEY

Muzot is the name of a hamlet in the Valais region of Switzerland and is also ascribed to its medieval tower, chateau de Muzot, perched above a small vineyard and inhabited by the poet Rainer Maria Rilke from 1919 to 1926. I first visited Muzot and the dramatic grave site of Rilke in nearby Raron in 1996 when I was researching the Rough Guide to Switzerland. Almost thirty years on there have been many changes to the surrounding landscape, in both locations and which, in Muzot's case, have made the immediate area of the tower a form of oasis, since it is thankfully protected, amidst the sprawl of development. I have often reflected on what the great poet who relished solitude and peace on this then quiet hillside would have made of these devastating urban changes, but we can be sure he would have been deeply wounded by them. Rilke was acutely sensitive to his surroundings, which were crucial in dictating whether he could work creatively and he was himself disparaging of the nearby ostentatious Chateau Mercier, built by a Swiss industrialist at the turn of the century, and steered well clear of it, seeing it as a vulgar modern intrusion lacking in authenticity. Now Mercier seems the least offensive edifice, as modern bungalows and luxury villas creep ever nearer the pastoral domain of Muzot. Now street lighting has been introduced to the tarmacked road which in Rilke's time was a dirt track taken by donkeys. This depressing evolution was symbolised during my last visit when I found a coke can tossed from the lane into Rilke's hallowed rose beds. It seemed to mark the end.

THE DEDICATION OF OTTO DIX

To render truthfully the skulls and corpses in his famous graphic series of *War Etchings* published in 1924, artist and ex-soldier of Flanders and the Somme Otto Dix travelled to Palermo during the winter of 1923 to visit the catacombs dei Cappuccini to study its renowned mummies. He made several striking drawings and gouaches of the deceased monks and other clergy still in their niches. These were incorporated into the scenes of human carnage he had personally witnessed on the battlefield. Dix was one of the most fanatical artists for communicating the undiluted truth, for him all other criteria were secondary.

RESISTANCE IN PARIS

Monique Saint-Hélier (1895–1955) was a Swiss French writer who as a young woman had met the poet Rainer Maria Rilke at a ball in Switzerland and, like so many falling under his spell, maintained a correspondence with him until his death in 1926.

Her later life was spent in a state of invalidity in Paris where, briefly fleeing the German advance on Paris in May 1940 aside, she barely left her rooms. A retinue of doctors were never to properly diagnose what her ailment was, but she still wrote determinedly from her bed or wheelchair a series of penetrating and sympathetic portraits of those writers and artists she had known during her more active life, most notably Rilke. She also wrote novels and stories which received much praise in her time, though after her death her reputation dissipated somewhat until the rediscovery of her work in the 1980s through the 'L'âge d'Homme' Swiss literature series.

The Author

WILL STONE is a poet, essayist and literary translator who divides his time between East Suffolk, Exmoor and the European continent. His first poetry collection *Glaciation* (Salt Publishing, 2007), won the International Glen Dimplex Award (Dublin, Ireland) for Poetry in 2008. Subsequent collections *Drawing in Ash* (Salt, 2011), *The Sleepwalkers* (Shearsman, 2016) and *The Slowing Ride* (Shearsman, 2020) have been critically appraised and all four are now available from Shearsman Books.

Will's translations from French and German include works by Stefan Zweig, Joseph Roth, Georg Trakl, Rainer Maria Rilke, Gérard de Nerval, Georg Simmel, Maurice Betz, Émile Verhaeren and Georges Rodenbach. His most recently published translations are *Letters around a Garden*, by Rainer Maria Rilke (Seagull Books, 2024) *Nietzsche in Italy* by Guy de Pourtalès (Pushkin Press, 2022) and *Bruges-la-Morte* by Georges Rodenbach (Wakefield Press, 2022). *Conversations with Rilke* by Maurice Betz will be published by Pushkin Press in 2025.

Will has contributed reviews, essays, poems and translations to a number of literary publications including the *Times Literary Supplement, London Magazine, The Spectator, Modern Poetry in Translation, Agenda, Irish Pages* and *Poetry Review*.